Weaned in the Desert:

Souvenirs from Sacred Seasons with my Savior

By: Genea Sheles Brice

PRESS

Preface

I have been writing all of my life. Poetry, plays, prose, essays, speeches, sermons, lesson plans, and the occasional thesis have all been a regular, frequent, and consistent part of my life, in some glorious form or another; for as long as I can remember. Whether mom was reciting the poetry of Psalms and Proverbs or dad was studying for a theme he would present on that Sunday morning, language, in all of its splendor, permeated our household like a most pleasant contagion.

In later years, my mother became a published poet and the fire of inspiration was ignited in me to an even greater degree. Here, then, is my contribution to the storehouse of literary expression. Receive it for what it is: one woman's treasure trove; line upon line, verse upon verse; a life-time of experiences straining to be contained in but a few pages. Such is the story of my life, really. For I have always felt too large for the space I occupied at any given time.

Though this Christian journey is to be taken seriously, to be sure, I am a firm believer that Christians should not take themselves too seriously! This accounts for the humorous tone of many of my heart musings. I believe that laughter doeth good like a medicine and let's face it: some days you just have to laugh to keep from crying!

Now, concerning the title: "Weaned in the Desert". What does it mean? Well, being the lexophile that I am, (lexophile meaning "lover of words") I find meaning in the letters that compose words and even in the spaces between the words on a page. I take pride in grammatical sentence structure, and even in the literary license to invent new ones! I find great joy in words and phrases, respectively. The oxymoron is particularly intriguing to me. I like the fact that in the English language we can juxtapose words or ideas that seem entirely different and create a new word or idea altogether. "Weaned in the Desert" became the title of this work because of its personal message to me.

When the Lord spoke the words "Weaned in the Desert", I was sitting in the Beauty Shop (on a side note, personal upkeep runs a close second behind spiritual upkeep in my book). While seated comfortably under the large hooded dryer, I prepared to study. It is my custom to schedule my hair appointments in conjunction with upcoming speaking engagements. My mind journeyed back to books I had read, to some experiences I had had, and to the Word of God which sustained me during some very hard and some extremely dry places in my life. The Spirit of the Lord said to me, "You are still here. Though it seemed like the bottom had fallen out from under you and hope was fading fast, I sustained you." He went on to say, "I was there—even in the desert." I began to weep unabashedly. I raised my hands in glorious praise to my worthy God, absolutely unconcerned about the fact that the shop was full of women, who I am sure, thought I was crazy. The Lord was saying, in essence, that weaning is the process by which parents remove something from a child in order to foster independence from it. This made sense.

The desert, of course, is a dry, desolate, arid place. So God, in His omniscience, was saying to me, "I, your loving father, have used the desert to remove some of your crutches. You have become too accustomed to living this way. I am using this dry, forbidding, lonely place to show you that I am all you need. I will now satisfy your mouth with good things. Trust me. You *will* grow here."

So, to those of you who may have found yourselves, all at once, scorched by the searing heat, frozen by the icy cold or awe-struck by the surprising beauty of your own desert, take courage. For it is here that you learn to make necessary adjustments for your continued survival. It is here that water can spring forth from some rather surprising sources. It is here that sustenance can be found where and when you least expect it.

It is my pleasure to share with you a sort of "view from my pew" as I journal my journey with Jesus. Come, traverse my treasured triumphs and feel the pain of all too frequent failings. Listen in on lessons learned from my Lord. See what I have seen, hear what I have heard, and feel what I have felt. And be encouraged, the desert is not so bad when you see it from God's perspective! For it was in the desert that he wooed the Children of Israel and loved them with an everlasting love. It was in the desert where he willingly betrothed them and took them as his bride. It was in the desert where he carried them as on eagles' wings out of bondage and suffering.

Now, if you still need a little more encouraging, take heart, I did, too! I will tell you like the Lord told me that day in the Beauty Shop: "Once you have been weaned in the desert, anywhere is an oasis; and when you cut your teeth on cactus, you can eat anything!"

Most Sincerely,

Genea S. Brice

Acknowledgements

To my loving and literary mother, Brenda Nell Mitchell-Walker, whose Godly example and unconditional love have given me both roots and wings! I love you more than I can adequately express. To my father, Archie Lee Green, whose humor and zest for life have proven to be indispensable staples for me. To my dear and doting daddy, Deacon Lloyd Walker, Sr., your faith in me means more than you know. To my siblings, thank you for giving me a deep well of happy times and fond memories from which I draw continually. Your contribution to my life is immeasurable. To my husband, the Reverend Larry W. Brice, Sr., who loves me at home and pastors me at church. To my children, Nicari and Larry, II, who never seemed to mind eating pop-tarts, popcorn and popsicles as I worked feverishly to bring this book to fruition.

Thank you.

Table of Contents

Life Lesson 1:

"Smile and Nod"

M y name is Genea Brice. If you had trouble pronouncing my first name, it's O.K., most people do. It's one of the many things I have had to get over in my life. And in the grand scheme of things, it is a small thing, to be sure! For your edification (put a mental pin right here, we'll be coming back to that word), my first name is pronounced /jen-ay/. I know it does not look like it. You would have guessed "Gina", you say. I know, it's O.K., now, back to "edification". Edification means, "The act of building up; encouraging." It's what we are supposed to be good at in The Body of Christ. (I Thess. 5:11). As the First Lady of a growing congregation in a large metropolitan city, I am supposed to be *really* good at it, right? Read on.

As God would have it, I am the instructor for the Young Women's Bible Study Group at our church. I know, "What an honor!" "Amen!" "Praise the Lord!" I'm happy about it now, but, believe me, God had to make it fit. I'll explain...

The number of young women joining our church had begun to grow exponentially. By "young" I mean women between the ages of 18 and 45. Although there was always Bible Study on Wednesday nights, they just didn't seem interested in the general forum. You don't have that problem at your church, I'm sure.

We noticed something started happening. We began to hear exciting conversation buzzing around the church. Women in this age group were busy talking about this wonderful new Bible Study Group they had found. In fact, every time a new young woman would join our church, she would almost instantly be recruited for the new Bible Study Group elsewhere. When enough women were mysteriously absent from goings on at our church and scheduled events were not so well-attended, pastor said, "Something will have to be done."

He went down on his knees and got up with a **revelation**, "We need a young women's class here!" He said. He called us (yes, *us*–which meant me, too), all together, gave his vision, and told us to pray for a teacher. Well, I was content to wait on God, and be faithful in our new class, under our new teacher, whoever it might be. My pastor/husband went back down on his knees and this time, got up with a **proclamation**: "Genea, it's you." Now, at this point, two things happened simultaneously. First, I fought back the desire to say like a certain '70's sitcom character would say to his older brother, "Whatchoo talkin' 'bout, Willis!?" Secondly, the desire to speak very sarcastically took over. "Who?!" I said, one eyebrow up, reminiscent of "Spock" from Star Trek. Before he could say another word, I continued to feign ignorance of this "Genea" person he seemed to be talking to and I looked behind me for an imaginary scapegoat, upon which to bestow this "honor". Since there was no such scapegoat or convenient ram in the bush, I determined to use my God-given gregariousness, natural spunkiness, and my college-educated teaching skills for the Glory of God, and the **edification** of my sisters. (Did you catch that?!) And besides, he wasn't letting up or backing down. He simply would not take "no" for an answer. Welcome to my world.

There were days when 30 women showed up and days when 5 showed up. There were days when they were disgruntled with me, and I with them. There were days when I was well received and days when I was not. There were even days when I was insulted, and felt like giving up. There were also days when I would receive an unexpected phone call encouraging me to "stay on the wall". Nevertheless, we have all been blessed in the process.

I have learned a lot in the years since I began teaching the class. Perhaps, the greatest lesson of all has been obedience. Obedience meaning not simply following directions, but the attitude with which you carry out such directions. It has been a tough lesson to learn, but necessary, none the less. As a result of God's grace and patience with me, I have incorporated a certain affirmation in our class. Now I teach my ladies when they are asked to do something on God's program, for God's people, just "Smile and Nod."

Souvenir: I Peter 4:9

"Use hospitality one to another without grudging."

Life Lesson 2:

"Cute and What Else?"

ℭℬ

As I grow more and more comfortable in my role as First Lady, I find myself coming in contact with a lot of different people in our church, particularly the women. Sunday mornings usually mean the customary greeting: "a virtual-kiss-on-the-cheek-because-we-don't-want-to-get-lipstick-on-each-other's-faces"; which is then followed by a polite hug so as not to muss each others' clothes. Sound familiar? Now, don't get me wrong… it isn't that the love is not genuine, it's just that we don't want to *mess- up* the *make-up*.

The Lord woke me up early one morning out of a sound sleep. You know the kind... you finally find that really warm spot and settle into it. Sleep comes and you embrace it like an old friend; fully intending to snore until your heart's content... Yes, that's the kind. Well, as I rubbed the vestiges of sleep from my eyes, The Lord began to speak to my spirit. He said, "Man looks at the outward appearance, but God looks at the heart." A bit perturbed, I sucked my teeth (you know that sound your children make when they really don't want to wash the dishes?) and responded, "Lord, I already know *that* Scripture," hoping the message would get more profound, after all, I *was* asleep. I began to mentally rehearse the scripture where the Children of Israel demanded a king of their faithful servant Samuel, and much to their future sorrow, ended up getting just what they desired. (I Sam. 8: 5, 6). It was in this story, that the Lord commanded Samuel not to be impressed by the physical appearance of Jesse's sons. Instead, he was to let the anointing do the talking.

The Lord continued to speak. He said, "Much preparation, time, effort, and energy is spent preening for Sunday mornings. The physical body is poised and polished, to be sure. But what of the inner man? What of the spirit? How much time goes into *truly* getting ready to come to my house? What of consecration? Worship? Koinonia?" Wide awake and fully attentive now, I said, "Speak Lord, for your servant hears." He continued, "Your influence must transcend suits, shoes, handkerchiefs, and hats. Tell the women it's O.K. to keep hair and nail appointments. It's O.K. to keep the body in shape. It's O.K. to eat well and keep up one's physical appearance, but tell them, "That's not all there is. (Bodily exercise profiteth little, remember?) They've got to be cute and something else!"

As I began to worship my worthy God in the wee hours of that morning, the tears flowed freely. Praise poured from my lips like welcome rains onto parched terrain. "Thank you, Lord!" I exclaimed. Grateful that He chose to impart such a word to me, I gladly received the revelation. In essence, God was saying to me, yea, to all of us, that there must be some depth to our walk with the Lord; depth that surpasses the outward appearance. The Lord must be so attractive to us on the inside, that He shows up on the outside. We should let our lights so shine before men that they will see our good works and glorify our Father who is in heaven. I determined

then and there that I would embrace my sisters genuinely, greet one

another with a holy kiss, and most of all, prepare the inner man for

worship of my worthy God!

Souvenir: I Peter: 3:3

"Let your adorning not be just the outward man…"

Life Lesson 3:

"Not on my Watch!"

℘

The fourth weekend in March is an exciting time for our church! Our pastor, under the guidance of the Holy Spirit, sanctioned this weekend to be set aside for our Annual Women's Conference. Two years ago, we began incorporating our young girls, ages 8-18, as well. Their night is Friday night. They participate in the program; singing, praise dancing, sign language selections, etc. It is great!

As God would have it, I have been called to be the kick-off speaker on that Friday night. What a blessing! Girls have been delivered, changes have been made, and decisions to follow Christ have been declared. Truly wondrous works have been wrought over this weekend. The Word of God is true; Jesus said, "And I, if I be lifted up from the Earth, I will draw all men unto me." He proves this over and over again over the course of this weekend.

One year, we chose for an overall theme, "Women of God: Laboring in the Vineyard". I struggled about just what to share with our young girls. What would be Relevant? Relateable? Real? The Lord said, ***"The Design of a Durable Daughter"***, taken from the story of Jairus' daughter in St. Mark 5:22-42. In my proclamation, I shared with the girls the importance of coming to one another's aid and helping; not spreading negative news. Unlike the negative people in the story who ran to tell Jairus that his daughter was already dead, thus possibly dashing his hopes and giving rise to unreasonable fear.

The Lord impressed upon my spirit the absolute necessity of encouraging one another in the church. I shared with them that night that our fellow sisters in Christ should not perish; they should not succumb to life's raging torrents and merciless storms; they should not quit the walk of life and die without those who care about them praying for them. We determined that night, that such a thing would not happen... "Not on my watch!" We should seek to edify, stir up, and encourage one another. Not to belittle, tear down, or discourage one another. Negativity surrounds us on every side; bad news seems to follow us, and it is sad to say, that often times, the most discouragement can come directly from one's own family. So it is in the Body of Christ; the family of God. We are often guilty of killing one another's joy, peace, and testimony, when we should be the ones most ready, willing, and able to lend a helping hand. Say with me resolutely: "My sister will not die—No, not on my watch!"

Souvenir: James 5:16

"Pray ye for one another..."

Life Lesson 4:

"Huponikeo: Just do It!"

❦

One day while meditating upon the Word of God, I came across a passage of Scripture that encouraged me so. Granted, it was familiar, and one I had heard countless times in Sunday School, Vacation Bible School and numerous Sunday morning sermons, alike, but that's what I love the most about the Word of God: it is remarkably relevant. It stays fresh, like it has been placed in a divine Ziploc baggy for all eternity! Don't you love that?! So, this passage holds beautiful promises for me even now. The Scripture read: "We are more than conquerors through Jesus

Christ who loved us." Just reading the words brought lilt to my life and joy for my doldrums.

Now, if I got all that encouragement just by **reading** the Word of God, imagine what happened when I actually **studied** it! I discovered that the English words "more than conquerors" are actually the one Greek word "huponikeo". The prefix "hupo" means "more than" or "over". "Nikeo" means "conquerors" or "winners". What blessed me was learning that we are not only winners and conquerors; but we are "more" than that. I was further illumined to discover that we are actually winners before the bell rings, before the gun goes off, and even before the flag drops. The fight is fixed! We win before we begin!! Does that not bless you?!

I do not, in any way, wish to minimize some of the trials and tribulations that plague us in this life. I am well aware of the fact that there are some things along this life's journey that can absolutely take the wind right out of our sails. There are some things that make it hard to go on. But just like it will always do, the Word of God is our anchor that keeps us stable and steadfast out on the restless sea of life. We are constantly and consistently reassured that even in our darkest hours, we can make it.

Someone knew this powerful truth and turned it into a multi-million dollar shoe and clothing empire called "NIKE". If you look closely at the word "huponikeo", you will find the word "Nike" smack dab in the middle. "Nike" is the name of the Greek goddess who personified triumph throughout the Greek ages. She is known as the "Winged Goddess of Victory". To the ancient Greeks, what could have been more important than winning, excelling, and conquering in the sports arena?! Brilliant! So, if the Greeks knew this truth, and multi-millionaire business moguls could capitalize on this truth, what about us as Children of God? Surely, we, too, can grab a hold of God's word and take it for what it says, "We are more than conquerors!" So...Just do it!!!

Souvenir: Matt. 17:20

"And nothing shall be impossible for you!"

Life Lesson 5:

"Thank the Lord for Carrot Cake!"

A s the Lord continues to use me in His service, I travel frequently. I have been invited to some awesome places throughout the state of California and the United States, respectively. It has been my high honor to stand in both illustrious pulpits before thousands as well as to share in intimate settings in Bible Studies. I have been blessed as well, to share God's word in conventions and conferences, alike. To God be the glory for the things He has done!!

I can recall on one occasion, I was at a convention to speak for three days. I had prepared my lessons, prayed and was ready. After attending the evening services with my assistant, we decided to get something to eat. Thinking this was somehow a novel idea, you can imagine my surprise when everyone in the auditorium had the same idea, and spilled out into the very same restaurant we had chosen. Mind you, I was new to the whole thing. As we grew closer to the restaurant, the line was long and the wait would be even longer. I didn't mind at all. I had something on my mind that made the wait entirely tolerable: carrot cake! I simply love it. I know; perhaps one should not use such a strong word to describe one's desire for a dessert, but I mean it: **I LOVE CARROT CAKE!!!!** Spotting the picture of a beautiful, large piece of carrot cake on the big menu posted on their wall, I was content in the knowledge that soon we would be together.

After waiting for a while, my assistant excused herself to take a phone call and I stayed behind to wait for her and to hold our place in line. Out of the corner of my eye, I could see the figure of a man standing a little ways off. After a few seconds, he seemed to get closer and closer to me. Aware of his presence but having no reason to acknowledge it, I kept up the small talk with the other people in line. Finally, he just walked right up to me and began speaking to me. "Hi. Are you here with the convention?" I answered, "Yes." He went on to say, "I have never seen you here before." Absolutely sure that someone could hear my stomach growling and grateful that we were next in line, I began to answer him. Just as I formed the words to respond, another teacher on program for the convention stepped up and replied, "Yes, that's Larry Brice's wife." The man who was once so curious left without another word.

After dining sufficiently on my carrot cake, my assistant and I went back to our rooms. After settling down to sleep, I awakened some time later. Something was on my mind. When I looked at the clock, it was 2:30 a.m. I knocked on my assistant's door. "Are you awake?" She mumbled, "No. What can I do for you?" I said, "I have a question. You remember earlier this evening, while we were standing in line…was that man trying to talk to me…you know, was he flirting with me?" "Yes, Sister Brice, he was. Anything else?" "No", I said. With that, I ran and jumped back on my bed. I called home. My husband answered the phone and said, "Is everything alright?" I said, "Yes, just tell the Lord, 'thank you'!" He said,

"Thank you, Lord". I hung up the phone, smiled, and was all at once even *more* grateful for carrot cake!! I was grateful that I had been so focused on the carrot cake that I did not even pay attention to the potential temptation that came my way. Grateful that even when I was not aware, others around me were. Grateful that God used carrot cake to keep my mind focused. I was grateful that the peripheral did not detract from the integral. The Lord will use even carrot cake to keep his people on the right track! Thank you Lord for carrot cake!!!

Souvenir: Isaiah 26:3

"Thou wilt keep him in perfect peace

whose mind is stayed on thee."

Life Lesson 6:

"When Wings Won't Work"

I was driving down the street coming from my cardio class and the Lord arrested my thoughts. I began to think about the past few years and all of the problems that seemed to characterize them. I began to speak to the Lord and He began to speak to me. I said, "Lord, why? Why were things so hard? Why are things so difficult now? What purpose did the pain serve?"

As the tears flowed, I heard the Lord speak directly to my heart. He said, "I saw you in your pain. I saw you when it hurt. I heard you when you cried. I even knew you wanted me to give you wings of a dove so you could just get far away from your situation. I knew you were tired mentally, physically and spiritually. I knew then and I know now. But here is the lesson: There will be times when you will soar as on eagles' wings of triumph. When everything you do will seem to work. There will be times when I will carry you on my wings, as I did the Children of Israel; out of bondage and out of suffering. There will be times when I will heal you with healing from my wings; when the sickness vanishes and the healing comes quickly. There will be times when waiting on me will cause you to mount up on wings as eagles. Times when I will be so pleased with your posture in waiting, that I will give you a bird's eye view of your future. There will be those times, to be sure. But there will be other times, as well. There will be times when wings won't work. There will be times when *mounting up* is not my will; but when *walking through*, is. There will be times in this life when you have to trust me even when you can't trace me; when you will just have to walk it out."

I began to rejoice then, because I got it. I began to understand why David said, "Yea, though I *walk* through the valley of the shadow of death, I will fear no evil..." Sometimes we will have to

Life Lesson 7:

"Palace Potential"

It is a beautiful thing to walk in *purpose*. It is wonderful to know what God has called you to do and to be able to watch as He unfolds that purpose in your life like the opening of rose petals. I know my purpose. I even had it printed on business cards: Genea S. Brice. Christian Conference Speaker. "Sharing God's word, With God's women, God's way." That's me. That's what I do.

In this capacity, I have been called on to minister to many different people in many different settings: Women's Annual Days, Appreciation Services, Conferences, Conventions, Military services, Bible Studies, seminars, lectures, and workshops, respectively. For this reason, it has been my honor to study the lives of women in the bible. There are those prominent women such as Ruth, Mary and Elizabeth, whose Godly examples resonate with us. There are notorious women such as Jezebel, Delilah, and Potiphar's wife, whose ungodly behavior serves to warn us against emulating their actions. Then there are those courageous women like Deborah, Rahab, and Jael, whose fearless devotion to God and his people caused them to rise to the occasion and defeat the enemies of Israel.

As God continues to open doors, he illumines His word for me and gives me a fresh understanding concerning the lives of Biblical women of the past and Christian women of today. Allow me to be transparent...

I am a wife, a mother, a teacher, and, as was stated previously, I am a First Lady. As I write this book, I am also poised to celebrate my fortieth (40th) birthday in a matter of months. I take care of myself. I try to eat right (with the exception of that occasional rather large slice of carrot cake, remember?), I exercise and I think I look pretty good (at least that's what the man at the gas station told me yesterday). All of this notwithstanding, I am a woman. A woman with flaws, downfalls, likes, dislikes, faults and failures too numerous to name. I love the Lord with all of my heart, mind, body and soul and yet, sometimes, I struggle with *knowing* what is right and *doing* what is right. Can I get a witness?! There are several women in Scripture who also struggled and whose examples encourage me greatly. One of the reasons I love the Word of God so much is because it is filled with ordinary people with ordinary failings, yet when used by God, they accomplish extraordinary things! One such woman was Esther.

Esther was a woman of great complexity. Seemingly overnight, she went from orphanage to opportunity. Esther had what I call **"Palace Potential"**. Though she was orphaned and had to be taken in by Mordecai, her older male cousin, she lacked nothing in the way of family love, concern, or guidance. Mordecai took great care of Esther. He loved her as if she were his own daughter.

As we encapsulate this great Bible story, we learn that this woman, with the aid of a caring father-figure, enters the Shushan beauty pageant to fill the vacancy left by Queen Vashti. Not only does she enter it, but she wins! She finds favor with the King, and he makes her queen instead of Vashti. Because of her new standing with the King, she is in prime position to fulfill her *ultimate purpose*: To save her people from utter destruction. I believe Esther is able to fulfill her destiny because of three (3) things:

I. Her Feet. According to Esther 5:1, she **stood** in the inner court of the king's house. It matters how *she* stood then and it matters how *we* stand now. Our standing in our homes, in our churches and in our communities at large, speaks volumes about what we profess concerning our Lord. She was in the right position. She was in the inner court. The inner court, as a matter of biblical history, represented closeness to God. It represented intimacy and privilege. If we are to please God, we, too, have to be close to him. Our attitude, that is, our standing, has to be right before the Lord.

II. Her Face. According to Esther 5:2, when the king **saw** her, she obtained favor in his sight. Now, for a bit of clarification. Verse 1 has to do with Esther's *spirituality*. That is to say, her standing before the *Lord*. I believe, then, that verse 2, has to do with Esther's *physicality*. That is to say, her standing before her *husband*. Men are visual and they notice a pretty woman. This is not a new revelation, to be sure, but one that bears emphasizing here. The King was absolutely smitten with Esther and it was clear that she was pleasing not only to his heart, (the Bible said he loved her), but she was also pleasing to his eye.

III. Her Faith. According to Esther 5:4, she speaks to the King and hints around at a request. She does not come right out and ask, mind you. Here, the bible shows us that she must have *faith enough* to believe that the King will be *intrigued enough* to take her up on her request.

Though Esther's story ends with her people being saved from genocide by "Haman the Hater", the Lord showed me something about her personality that bears noting. Even though she had been told of the plot to have her people killed, Esther was not exactly "chomping at the bit" to jump right in and help. After all, she had entered the beauty pageant against *all* of the other beautiful virgins in the entire province *and won*! After all, she had not only won first place, but she had also won the King's heart! Shouldn't she be allowed to bask in the special glow of victory? Shouldn't she be able to rest on her laurels? Shouldn't she be allowed to savor the spoils of victory? Because, now, as everyone knew, she was the queen. Just as this attitude was beginning to take root, she gets a message from Mordecai. He reminded her of her true purpose. He began to show her the "big picture". Mordecai had to remind her that winning the beauty pageant and being crowned "Shushan's Next Top Model", if you will, were merely a means to an end. Her true purpose was to use her position to save her people. Mordecai, in the way that only a loving, caring and stern father can, causes her to think about something: He says to her in Esther 4:13 and 14, and I paraphrase: "Look, girly, girl. Don't get the "big head" and lose sight of the "big picture". Just because you are sitting up there in that big palace now, comfortable and safe behind those tall walls, don't get it twisted: you still have a job to do. When this news breaks, you, too, will be in jeopardy. What makes you think that you will be saved? Don't forget you are a Jew, too. So, if you decide to be quiet and do nothing, even though you are in a position to help, God is still able to save his people and he can use any means to do it. But who knows? I believe this is why you were called into the kingdom; for such a time as this." In other words, Mordecai shook Esther out of her false sense of security and self-sufficiency. He effectively ushered her right into her desert of dependence on God and his providence.

In that desert she fasted for three (3) days without food or water. She prayed that God would do the absolute impossible, and he did. Because of Esther's desert experience, her people were saved. There is purpose in the desert!

Souvenir: Esther 4:14

"...and who knoweth whether thou art come to the kingdom for such a time as this?"

Life Lesson 8:

"Hope for Hagar"

One of my most favorite bible lessons came about as a result of studying for a Women's Conference I was to conduct some years ago. I had been praying about what to say to this particular group of women, and in my time of consecration and meditation, I heard the Lord say, "Encourage them. Let them know that their faults and failures are forgiven. Tell them that I still love them and will continue to provide for them. There will be no sister left behind." Well, you know what happened next…I fell out on the floor weeping and blessing God for such beautiful reassurance. I have found out from years of studying God's word, that the word you think you are imparting to others, will first be imparted to you. God is awesome, isn't he? Hagar is another woman whose story speaks volumes to me.

The Lord led me to the story of Hagar found in Genesis 16. As the story unfolds, we discover that we are quite familiar with the details of this young woman's life and how she fits in the life of Abram and Sarai. Admittedly, it is a peculiar puzzle, indeed. We know that God had promised Abram a son in his old age and that this son would come through both Abram and his wife Sarai. Because of a toxic combination of impatience, a lack of faith, and a warped belief that one can actually "help" the plan of God along, Hagar becomes pregnant by Abram, at Sarai's urging. (Wow.) As I studied this passage of Scripture, I took a closer look and discovered four (4) pertinent points that highlight Hagar's story:

I. **Hagar's Precarious Situation.** (Genesis 16: 1-4). The word "precarious" means "dependent upon the will or favor of another; uncertain or risky." We learn in Genesis 16:1 that Hagar is Sarai's handmaid, or servant. That is to say, Hagar lives and exists at the whim and will of her mistress Sarai. Hagar has no voice and therefore, she has no choice. She simply must do as she is told. She serves only to please the lady of the house. Her situation is quite clearly precarious, indeed. So, it is little wonder then, why Hagar agreed to the plan of her mistress Sarai, when she insisted that she sleep with Abram in order to produce the promised heir. (Well, now).

II. Hagar's Presumptuous Son. (Genesis 21:9,10). The word "presumptuous" means "overstepping one's bounds; being too bold or forward; showing overconfidence or taking too many liberties." By the time we get to chapter 21 in this "love triangle", if you will, we find that the son is born. In fact, his name is Ishmael and most scholars believe he is about sixteen years old. He is a young man now. The other interesting development was the earlier birth of Isaac, the promised son. Now, get the picture: in the same house we have the son of promise, Isaac, living along side the son of promiscuity, Ishmael. What fun they must have had at holidays! Lest I digress, let's get back to the story. Well, in verse 9 of chapter 21, Sarah notices something. She catches Ishmael—the son of the slave girl—teasing and mocking her son Isaac. Ishmael takes a little too many liberties and in Sarah's eyes, goes too far. Now he has to go. I can just hear Sarah reasoning to herself, "I mean, how dare this boy tease and mock the promised child of Abraham (notice that their names were changed in chapter 17) the patriarch. Just who does he think he is?! Now, he's got to go and his mama, too!"

III. Hagar's Precious Savior. (Genesis 21: 17, 18). Well, you know how the story goes: Abraham casts Hagar and Ishmael away at the insistence of Sarah. While he did kick them out, it is interesting to note that the Bible says in chapter 21, verse 11 that this thing was "very grievous" in his sight because of his son. It is clear that Abraham loved Ishmael. It doesn't say anything about it being "very grievous" in his sight because of Hagar, mind you, but he *did* love his son. So, they are on their way. Abraham got up early in the morning, gave them some bread and a bottle of water (that they were supposed to *share*!) and off they went. The bible says in verse 14, that she departed and wandered in the **wilderness** of Beersheba. Here she is. Driven out into the wilderness by Abraham, yet, at the same time, driven into her desert by the omniscient hand of God. The miracle comes in verses 16-18. Just as she is poised to *give up* and despair because there is no more water and she has no idea how she will provide for herself, let alone, provide for her son, God *shows up*. In verse 17, the Bible says, "And God heard the voice of the lad; and the angel of God called to Hagar out of heaven and said unto her, 'What aileth thee, Hagar? Fear not; for God hath heard the voice of the lad where he is." Verse 18 goes on to say, "Arise, lift up the lad, and hold him in thine hand; for I will make him a great nation. And God opened her eyes..." Are you shouting yet? I am! He was aware of her; he was aware of her situation and he let her know in no uncertain terms, that everything would be alright!!

IV. Hagar's Portion Supplied. (Genesis 21:19, 20). So, here she is. Helpless, homeless and desperate. Having left the only home she had ever known and, perhaps, the only man she had ever loved. But just like he will do every time, God showed up. In verses 19 and 20, the Bible says, "And God opened her eyes, and she saw a well of water; and she went, and filled the bottle with water, and gave the lad drink. And God was with the lad;

and he grew, and dwelt in the wilderness, and became an archer."

Abraham gave her a bottle, but God gave her a well!!! Who needs a bottle when God can give you a well?! God fulfilled in verse 20, what he promised in verse 18. He is a God of his word. Because of Hagar's connection to Abraham, Ishmael was blessed. Her portion of the promise was supplied! God made of the bondwoman's son a great nation! Lesson: No matter where you may find yourself in this life; no matter what circumstances you may be facing, you can never go wrong when you lean on the promises of God! He sees, He knows, and He cares. His unseen hand is always working in the background; His ears are attentive to the cry of his people, and He will move swiftly on our behalf!

Yes, there is hope, yes, even for Hagar!! God provided for her *in the desert*! He encouraged her *in the desert*! He saved her, yes, *in the desert*! He let her know that everything would be alright **<u>RIGHT THERE IN THE DESERT</u>**!! I have learned that God becomes dear in the desert!!!! Bless His name!!

Life Lesson 9:

"Favor"

ಞ

A couple of years ago, I was blessed to speak at our church on a Sunday morning. This particular Sunday morning was special in that we were closing out the Annual Women's Conference, started some years earlier. The women were all excited, having experienced Shekinah Glory all weekend long. Our theme for this particular year was "Women of God: Walking in the Favor of God!" What a theme! What a concept! What a blessing!

I had shouted all weekend long and as a result, I had no voice left at all. All that would proceed from my mouth were harsh-sounding whispers and something that resembled croaking. I tried to convince my husband that I would not be disappointed if he just went ahead and preached that morning. He was having none of it. I told him I was hoarse and that I just could not pull it off. He said in that dry, Texas drawl, "You'll be alright." That was it. So I sat there in my seat, praying for a voice. There were guests. Lots of guests. This *was* the close out of our fifth annual women's conference. And I had no voice. I was to bring the morning message and I had no voice. Man, oh, man.

Service proceeded along very well. The spirit of the Lord really reigned in that place. While in the midst of fighting a weird combination of fear, incompetence, and serious resentment of my husband, I heard my husband introducing me. Prayer replaced panic just as he called me up. I put all my weight on God, for He, alone, would have to carry me through. I am delighted to report that He did. It was a blessing!

I spoke from the passage of Scripture that houses the story of Cain and Abel. From this story, The Lord bestowed grace enough for me to give four (4) points concerning "Favor". I pray you are enlightened and edified as you read them below:

I. <u>Favor is often Unknown at first</u>. According to Genesis 4: 1 and 2, Adam and Eve had two sons named Cain and Abel. Cain was a farmer and Abel was a shepherd. At this point, the Bible makes no distinction between the two of them, except that they have two different occupations. It is not until two verses later that we will come to know their spiritual differences, which will prove to be most significant, to be sure.

II. <u>Favor is always Undeserved by us.</u> In verse 3, we get a glimpse of worship. The bible says that "in the process of time it came to pass, that Cain brought of the fruit of the ground an offering unto the LORD." Verse 4 reads, "And Abel, he also brought of the firstlings of his flock and of the fat thereof. And the LORD had respect unto Abel and to his offering:" Here, we discover that favor is upon the life, and, therefore, on the offering of Abel. While this is true, we must first understand that favor and who gets it, is entirely up to God. I appreciate our leaders in the body of Christ. One great preacher in particular said something that resonates with me and helps prove the point here: "Favor ain't Fair!" Many scholars have speculated as to why God favored Abel's offering and not Cain's, but all I know is that the bible said he did. That's it and that's all. We do know that favor is a gift bestowed upon us by God and that we can, in no way, earn it and neither do we deserve it; we can never take credit for it or find ourselves boasting about it. It is simply the Lord's doing, and it is marvelous in our eyes!

III. Favor is Unappreciated by the world. The fact that Abel's offering had been accepted by the LORD, should have been a time of celebration and praise. Abel should have been able to share his blessing with his brother, and Cain should have entered into his brother's joy. But Cain was anything but happy for Abel. Verse 5 gives us great insight into the psyche of Cain. It reads, "But unto Cain and to his offering he (God) had not respect. And Cain was very wroth, and his countenance fell." This is a picture of a jealous person who will not be dissuaded. Perhaps he was embarrassed or saddened, but we know for sure that he was angry. Anger burned within him like hot coals of fire, refusing to cool. Cain did not view Abel's acceptance by God as a learning experience; something from which he could learn and grow, no.

He viewed it as a personal affront and insult against him. He would not be comforted.

IV. <u>Favor is Unmistakable by all.</u> Although Cain did not understand nor appreciate Abel's worship to God, God, himself, did. God put his "stamp of approval", if you will, upon Abel's sacrifice. It was unmistakable. God spoke it. God blessed it. God was pleased with Abel. What I love about God is that he is no respecter of persons. He lets us know that it is not Abel that is so right and Cain that is so wrong. We find this in verse 6: "And the LORD said unto Cain, why art thou wroth? And why is thy countenance fallen? He continues in verse 7, "If **thou** doest well, shalt thou not be accepted?" God is letting Cain know that his offering; his worship can be acceptable to. Try again. Learn of me, he says. Learn what I will accept and do likewise. God was giving Cain another chance to get it right. But, he just could not get over the fact that his offering was unacceptable while his brother's was.

Abel's favor was unmistakable. God was so pleased with Abel, that his story made it in the book! Favor is bestowed upon us at the sheer will and desire of God Almighty. And sometimes, as Abel's example shows us, it will cost us everything to walk in the favor of God. I am a witness.

Souvenir: II Corinthians 9:15

"Thanks be unto God for his unspeakable gift."

Life Lesson 10:

"The Wisdom of Wonder Woman"

℘

As I have mentioned previously, I am a First Lady. That is to say, my husband is the pastor of a church. This comes with its own unique challenges, to be sure. One day while I was bemoaning my state, and wondering why life is so hard, the Lord centered my attention on television shows of the 1970's and the surprising wisdom found therein. It is amazing what God will use to illuminate truths for His glory, isn't it? Watching shows like Happy Days, Good Times, The Jefferson's, Laverne and Shirley and Mork and Mindy were a regular part of my family's evening routine. While these shows were good, four (4) of them were my favorites. The first in the list is Wonder Woman. There are two (2) very specific examples I have gleaned from the life of Diana Prince a.k.a. Wonder Woman that helped me get through "a particularly rough patch of road".

I. "The Invisible Jet". I have learned that it is absolutely necessary to possess something that is invisible to the naked eye, but it keeps you flying high! Wonder Woman had an invisible jet that transported her swiftly from one place to another. She knew it was there, but no one else could see it. So it is in the life of Christian women today: we must possess that special something that keeps us afloat amid the sometimes treacherous waters of life. We must be able to call upon something that will lift us out of whatever slump, funk or mess we are in; whether of our own making or not. Others won't know it; others won't be able to see it and they most certainly won't understand it. They won't understand why you praise God anyway. Even when all hell is breaking loose and nothing is going as planned. The Christian woman relies on that one peculiar, indispensable, invisible Helper called the Holy Spirit to raise her up. The Lord encouraged me with the words of the Psalmist: "When my heart is overwhelmed, lead me to the

Rock that is higher than I!" I can go to the Rock that is higher than I! I can lean and depend on the Rock that is higher than I. I am able to transcend current circumstances. I can be instantly transported out of gloom, doom, and frustration, because God always makes a way of escape!

II. "It's all in the Accessories!" Now, as I stated earlier, I believe personal upkeep runs a close second behind spiritual upkeep. It's a good thing, too, because historically, in the Black church, one of the unspoken job descriptions outlined for the First Lady is that of "Fashion Mogul". Traditionally, it was the First Lady who set the fashion tone for the congregation (whether by overt action or accidental choice that morning). What she wears speaks volumes about who she is. I didn't create the rule, but I do know it exists. Remember Wonder Woman's outfit? She wore that patriotic red, white, and blue sort-of-swimsuit-get-up that was set off by those nifty knee boots. Remember that gold stripe that ran up the middle? And what set off that gold stripe? Those gold bracelets! They deflected bullets *and* brought her whole ensemble together. Fashionable and functional! You remember, don't you?! Now, I am not suggesting that the pastor's wife show up at church on Sunday morning wearing a patriotic swimsuit. That would be funny, wouldn't it?! Can you imagine? It would be all over! What I am suggesting is that we take a page from Wonder Woman on this wise: her name is *Wonder* Woman. She was able to hold down a good government job, soar head and shoulders above the rest, keep those she cared for safe from harm, and all while being spit-shined and polished— with perfect hair, no less! Sounds like a First Lady to me!

Lesson: Keep yourselves up, ladies. Keep your hair and nail appointments. Get massages, go on vacations. Life is too short to look bad. Keeping all of this advice in mind, we must never lose focus of the fact that the true beauty of the First Lady does not come from what she wears on the outside, but it comes from who she is on the inside. She must put on the whole armor of God, so that she may be able to stand in the evil day.

<u>Souvenir: Proverbs 31:30</u>

<u>*"Favor is deceitful, and beauty is vain: but a woman*</u>

<u>*that feareth the LORD, she shall be praised."*</u>

Life Lesson 11:

"Incredible Insights from the Incredible Hulk"

The second example featuring television shows from the 1970's is The Incredible Hulk. It was one of my all time favorites. I was enthralled as Bill Bixby turned into Lou Ferrigno, who turned into the Hulk. I could not be deterred. That was my show. Remembering this show helped me during a misunderstanding that could have quickly gotten out of hand. Let me explain:

My first year at our new church found me all at once both anxious and curious. I so wanted to "be about my father's business". I wanted to meet people and begin the work of ministry.

Getting involved with ministries and being a part of something greater than myself appealed to me immensely. Parenthetically, I am a rather exuberant person by nature; I love people and I embrace life with both hands, intending to live it to the fullest (even as I write this, I am smiling from ear to ear). I also tend to believe in the best in people. I was in store for some rather abrupt reality checks, courtesy of our new assignment.

One day, a particular ministry was putting on a program and I was asked to lend a helping hand. The day came and I was ready. At the time, my daughter was only two years old, so I brought her along with me. The person in charge came to me and said, "Sis. Brice, we are going to need your help. You can put your daughter in the office with a video and a pizza." Now, as you can imagine, I paused to make sure I heard her correctly. I mentally pressed rewind and played it again. Yes, that's what she said. Well, my heart started pounding, my pulse was racing and I could feel heat rising from somewhere near my toes, creeping up my neck, and resting on the top of my head. I wanted to say in the immortal words of Dr. Bruce Banner, "Don't make me angry. You wouldn't like me when I'm angry."

Now, here's the lesson I learned that day: No matter how nice, sweet, calm, cool, and collected we think we are; no matter how nicely put together we appear, and no matter how subdued and serene we may start out, no one is perfect. No one, no, not even the First Lady. We all possess the potential to act in some very un-Christian-like ways. I hate to admit it, but I was really about to go smooth off and tell that lady where to go and how to get there! I mean, how dare she presume to tell me what to do with my daughter and on top of that, make such an asinine suggestion as to put a two year-old in an office alone...with an entire pizza?!?!! The nerve! I was angry. No, let me re-phrase: **I WAS HEATED**!! And at that moment, I needed something greater than myself to control myself. I needed something greater than myself to control my thoughts, my hands, and my tongue. I was made instantly aware of this truth: Without the indwelling of the Holy Spirit in the life of the believer, we simply cannot live a life pleasing to the Lord, no, not even the First Lady. I learned that day that there truly is a war in my members and when I would do good, evil is present with me. It is the power

of the Holy Ghost that makes living for the Lord possible. The Holy

Spirit is both a restrainer and a constrainer who allows us to over-

come without unleashing the monster within.

<u>Souvenir: Romans 7:18</u>

<u>"For I know that in me (that is in my flesh,)</u>

<u>dwelleth no good thing..."</u>

Life Lesson 12:

"Worth More than Six Million Dollars"

❧

I can remember sitting in our living room as a child, glued to the T.V. set watching another one of my favorites: The Six Million Dollar Man. I knew it was about to begin when on the screen bellowed great black balls of smoke and huge plumes of fire climbed ever higher into the sky. Steve Austin's rocket ship had just collided with the ground. He lies there clinging to life. Then come those familiar words…"Steve Austin….a man barely alive. We can re-build him…", spoken by that faithful helper, Oscar Goldman. I was hooked! Every week, you could find me at the same time, in the same place.

This scene came rushing back to me as I recall an incident in my life not long ago. It was one of those Sundays when I was finding it hard to praise. Not because God had somehow become less worthy that day, mind you, but because of "stuff". The morning had been difficult, the children were moving much too slowly, my husband was complaining, and, of course, we were running late-again. By the time I got to church, I was, quite frankly, spent. I must admit, I did not hear one note the choir sang that day, I cannot tell you what the sermon was about, and if the deacons prayed, I just hope they prayed for me. I had had it that day. I had begun rehearsing failures and set-backs that had been buried in an all-too shallow grave. Out of utter desperation and sheer exasperation, I cried out unto the Lord from somewhere deep within. It was then that the Spirit of the Lord came quietly and spoke deep into my soul, he said, "I know you don't feel like it, but you are valuable to me. I have entrusted great treasure in earthen vessels. I have entrusted you with my word. I could have used anything to share my word concerning my son, but I have chosen you. You are most valuable to me. I am going to use your story for my glory. This, too, shall pass." It was then that the words of Oscar Goldman came, by way of the Holy Spirit: "We can re-build her. She can be better than she was before. Better. Stronger. Faster."

If you recall the series, Steve Austin was given a new eye, new legs, and a new arm that cost a fortune; six million dollars, to be exact. By the aid of the Holy Spirit, that day, I got something new as well; and it cost Jesus his life. I got a new perspective; I had to stop viewing God's worth in the light of present circumstances. God is God and he is good ALWAYS. Even on a bad day, he is still good! He gave me a new song; He began to soothe my spirit with biblical truths that seemed to wipe away the frustrations of that morning. He gave me a new praise; I had to remember that praise is a debt we owe God and it is not dependent upon how we feel! I had to remember that everything that has breath should praise the Lord. I was changed.

I determined never again to sit in a church service with closed lips. I had to remember that if any man be in Christ, he is a new creature. I was valuable to the Lord. He told me so.

Souvenir: II Corinthians 4:7

"But we have this treasure in earthen vessels..."

Life Lesson 13:

"Trust the Voice on the Other End"

℘

I t was virtually impossible to live in the 1970's without expe-riencing the ubiquitous presence of Charlie's Angels! Lunch boxes, posters, dolls, hair-do's, and clothing styles all had the unmis-takable mark of Charlie's Angels.

Looking back secularly, the show worked because it was fun and flirty. We all agree that Farrah Fawcett, Jacqueline Smith, and Kate Jackson were beautiful women. The fact that they portrayed women who were strong, courageous, and skilled in police work, was also a plus for young girls coming of age in the '70's. This notwithstanding, the Lord used this show to drive home some spiritual truths for me as well:

I. Training is Essential. When Charlie's Angels first came on, we would hear that tell-tale music. Then we would hear the voice of Charlie explaining what was going on. He begins... "Once upon a time, there were three little girls who went to the police academy..." Scenes depicting them functioning in various capacities flashed on the screen. One would be walking children across the street as a crossing guard. Another would be answering phones, and still another would be practicing Judo moves in a class. It all looked very exciting! I assure you, there were many a day when I practiced some of those Judo moves on my unsuspecting siblings, much to their chagrin. But as the Lord had me focus on this show, he said, "Look deeper." I did. He revealed that they did not start off in a glamorous office. They did not always have a faithful assistant named Bosley. They had not always had nice cars and clothes. No. They had to work very hard and they had to be prepared for what would lie ahead. The Lord explained that we all want ease and comfort. We tend to disdain the menial tasks that often accompany Christian ministry, but greatness comes with time. To highlight this point, he reminded me of David. Though he was anointed to be king, he did not ascend the throne immediately. It took time. He had to serve his father, his brothers, and even a mad man named Saul. He had to endure unwarranted jealousies, he had to run for his life, and even hide out in caves. He was no less anointed. He was no less chosen. Life Lesson: God will manifest his *will* in His *time*. Wow!

II. Tune your Ear. The entire premise of "Charlie's Angels" fascinated me. I was intrigued by the fact that not only would these three (3) beautiful and intelligent women listen to this invisible voice on the other end of an intercom, but they would actually carry out his bidding, unquestioningly. What was it about this "Charlie" person? As I waited for the Lord to enlighten me, he did. He said, "Take a page from their book." I looked deeper. The Lord was showing me that the entire series was about faith. It centered around three women who completely trusted in a man they could not see. Are you shouting yet?! They had to trust him, though they could not trace him! They had to believe that he had their best interest at heart. So it is with us, as Christians. We are told in Hebrews 11:6 "But without faith it is impossible to please God: for he that cometh to God must believe that he is and that he is a rewarder of them that diligently seek him." To receive anything from God, we must first believe that he exists. Though we cannot see him, we must believe he is there. That invisible hand that works all things together for our good. That unseen friend who comforts us when we are lonely, who forgives our failures, and takes us from one good degree of grace to another. Just how is it that things worked out so well for "Charlie's Angels" at the end of every episode? Because they had their ears tuned only to the voice of the man on the other end of the intercom. Life Lesson: They *knew* only his voice, which meant they *trusted* only his voice, and, therefore, they *followed* only his voice. The Lord expects no less from us.

Souvenir: St. John 10:3-5

"...and the sheep hear his voice: and he calleth his own sheep by name, and leadeth them out...another they will not follow..."

Life Lesson 14:

"A Star Trek Moment"

ఇ

W ell, by now, we are well into our examination of television shows of the 1970's. I have one more I would like to share with you: Star Trek. Complete with cool outfits, futuristic gizmos and gadgets; funky hair and dramatic make-up; techno-music, and dazzling camera effects, who didn't love it?! Now, let me start off by saying that I am not a "Trekkie", but I did enjoy watching the show! "Captain Kirk", "Sulu", "Bones", "Uhura", "Scottie" "Spock", along with the other characters, fascinated us week after week, as they traveled around the universe confronting strange new worlds and solving space-age problems. This show would shed some light on an experience I had as I prepared for an upcoming engagement.

On one particular occasion, I was asked to speak for a women's annual day. This was my first time at this church, so I was not familiar with the environs. As is my custom, I enquired of our escort a place in which to compose myself and pray prior to entering the services. As we walked to a little room adjacent to the sanctuary, I immediately felt the Spirit of the Lord. I lifted my hands and began to worship him for yet another opportunity to speak for Him. I was all at once, overwhelmed by his grace and mercy toward me. I continued to worship my worthy God as we entered the room. I could hear the Lord saying, "I am pleased with you. It is not anything in your flesh that causes me to bless you, but it is your heart. You are chasing after me and I am pleased." Such knowledge was too great for me. Even as I share this, I am transported back to that very day and am overwhelmed all over again. Mentally, I frequent that place often, it comforts me.

As I began to compose myself and make ready to enter the sanctuary, I took a good look at the church. It was HUGE. There were chandeliers, plush carpeting, and it had a seating capacity of over 5,000 people. There were several large buildings including a gymnasium, a bookstore, café, and family life center. A separate wedding chapel, audio-visual booths, an orchestra pit, business offices, libraries, and ministries to meet the needs of the masses, covered the campus of this beautiful church. Now, I was overjoyed *and* overwhelmed! I began to ask the Lord, "Lord, how is it that I am here? Surely there are others who are more qualified, better educated or who have more impressive credentials than I. How is it that I have come to be here?" The Lord said to me, "This is only the beginning. I have great things in store for you. If you cry unto me I will show you great and mighty things that you have not known. Trust me. There are greater things ahead." Allow me to put it in my own words: In essence, the Lord was saying to me: "Get a Star Trek Moment." Get courage enough to "*boldly* go where no one has gone before!"

Just be strong and very courageous because there is more to see, more to share and more to accomplish for the kingdom! Ask the Lord for a "Star Trek Moment!"

Life Lesson 15:

"What Toby Taught Me"

When I was in the eleventh grade, we had a dog named Toby. He was a shiny black Labrador retriever with a vibrant white patch on his chest, just under his chin. He was beautiful. He was truly a family dog. We played with him, fed him, watered him, and even though he was not very big, we came to rely on him as our watch dog. Toby stayed in the backyard, faithfully keeping an eye out. The low, melodic tone of his barking assured us he was there.

One day, I came home and noticed Toby wasn't in the backyard. I looked around and couldn't find him. I asked my mother where he was and she didn't know. "Don't worry about it, he'll be back."

Mildly comforted, I went about the afternoon's duties. As night crept

in, cloaking the sky, there was still no sign of Toby. There wouldn't

be any sign of him for four days.

On the fourth day, when I came home from school, I went down

the back steps to the backyard just as I had done for the previous

three days. I noticed small, circular red drops on the white steps, on

the landing, on the ground and in the grass. I knew it was blood, but

where was it coming from? Panicked, I went down into the base-

ment. I found Toby lying there, with glassy, sunken eyes. I could

see his ribs through his once shiny black coat, which was now dull

and dirty. Tears welled up in my eyes as I watched my dog list-

less, hungry and so obviously in pain. I looked at his paws. They

were cut and bleeding. I ran in the house and told my mother Toby

was back, but he was sick and hurt. I began dashing around looking

for ointments and rags. I was going to fix him up. I was absolutely

mortified at what happened next. My mother said, "Leave him

alone." I cocked my head to the side and just looked at her. Didn't

she hear me? She continued, "He came back earlier today. I watched as he limped to the backyard. Don't do anything, just watch." Now, stunned, I wondered who this lady was standing in front of me. She looked like my mother, but she sounded like another. Who was this woman? She couldn't be my mother. My mother takes in strays of all kinds; from pets to people. What was going on here? When did my mother become so uncaring and callous? Reading the look on my face, she replied, "Trust me."

Later that night just before I turned out the light, I could hear the familiar sounds of Toby moving around. But what was he doing? I looked out my window and watched. He bent his head low to the ground and began chewing. Unsure of just what he was eating, I looked a little closer. He was eating the grass. He would eat, lie down, drink a little water and repeat the process. I didn't understand what was going on, but I determined I would investigate the next day.

The following day when I came home from school, I was surprised to find Toby up, running around and wagging his tail like always! What was this? My mother went on to explain: "Grass has medicinal properties for dogs. It is important to leave them alone, as this is the first stage of self-healing for them. We don't know where he has been; we don't know how he got hurt, and it doesn't matter. When dogs are ill, they should be allowed to get quiet, eat, and heal."

Wow. This episode flashed before me as I was once again at a low point in my life. The Lord began to speak volumes to me about this. Here is what Toby taught me:

I. The world is Unkind. It can be a cruel, harsh place. We will find that at times, we are no match for its punishing blows. When the world is unkind, however, we can always come back home. Running or limping, we can come back to the open arms of our Lord. When we are hurting because of heavy burdens and bleeding hearts, God is still there, right where we left him. I am reminded of the prodigal son. After he had run out of money, friends, and frivolity, he came back. He came running back home to the open arms of his loving father. We can, too!

II. Be Undisturbed. Solitude is invaluable. According to health care professionals, solitude can both precede and expedite healing. There is something remarkable about the sanctuary of silence. I have found that God often times does his best work in the quiet times. When our souls are truly ailing, the words of others can sometimes drown out the words of our God. We need only to hear from Him, and this is best accomplished when we are alone. I am reminded of Elijah when he was desperately alone and running from Jezebel. It was here that the voice of the Lord came to him. Not in the earthquake or the whirlwind, but in a still, small voice, bringing peace to a chaotic situation. It is the voice of God that stops the busy traffic that traverses in our minds. It is good, nay, it is mandatory, to get alone and get with God.

III. Eat Unhindered! Toby ate when he was sick. He ate when he was in pain. It has been my experience that in times of crisis, we tend to go to extremes as it relates to eating. Either we lose our appetites completely, and refuse to eat, or we over indulge and find ourselves bingeing. But the Lord showed me something very profound. He showed me that it is not only important that we eat at stressful times, but it is also important just what we eat. The Word of God is described as many things for us throughout Scripture. It is described as our light and our lamp. But the word picture I love the most, is The Bread of Life. It means that the word of God provides sustenance and nourishment when we are starved by the world's steady diet of indifference, hostility, and animosity. The Lord reiterated his promise to me: "He who eats of this bread will never hunger again." Like David who ate after the death of his child, we, too, are encouraged to eat. The Lord showed me that He is in control and will make it all turn out for our good in the end. Praise God! We don't have to lose our appetites when we are down, in fact, the down times should serve to whet our appetites for the necessary nutrients found in the Word of God! Eat up! As a side note, we did take Toby to the vet. He was given some fluids and a good bath. He was fine!!

Souvenir: St. John 6:35

"And Jesus said unto them, I am the bread of life:

he that cometh to me shall never hunger..."

Life Lesson 16:

"The Kelly Green Suit"

My husband set aside the second Sunday in November for an appreciation service for our assistant pastor and his wife. It was a pleasure to do this for them, as they had been faithful throughout their years of service. It was even more of an honor to celebrate them because they were my husband's brother and his wife.

Many thoughts filled my mind in preparation for that day. I would have to pick out the perfect gift for my sister-in-law and would encourage the ladies in the church to do the same. I would also have to pick out an appropriate outfit, of course. I had just the one in mind. Months earlier, I purchased a gorgeous suit. It was a fully lined, Kelly green wool suit, with brown fur around the collar and the cuffs! I know. You are speechless, too! To top that off, I purchased it in July, so it was a steal of a deal!!! I hadn't worn the suit because I needed to pick out the perfect shoes. Can't wear the suit without the shoes! Can I get a witness?!

One day I was in my favorite department store looking for a blouse. While strolling through the shoe department (I can't really recall how I got to that shoe department...), something green caught my eye. I tried to hide my enthusiasm, yet I seemed to be floating in the direction of those shoes. As I got closer, I got a good look at them: They were Kelly green, pointed-toe sling backs with—and this is the clincher—a brown wooden heel!!!!! It was like angels started singing and a light from the heavens shone down directly upon those beloved shoes. I picked one up, held it close to my chest, and I believe a tear formed in the corner of my eye. Sold! I did not get a blouse that day, but I did get those shoes. I was set for the second Sunday in November!

"Did you hear that?!" It started to appear that the Lord was reneging

on our deal. As I turned back around, all set to resume my clap-

ping and rocking, something happened. Tears began to fall down

my cheeks. Hands that were clapping were now lifted in praise, and

before I knew it, I was on the floor, face down, prostrate, worshiping

my worthy God! Like a river, thanksgiving poured from my lips. I

thanked Him for keeping me safe while riding in my car, I thanked

him for allowing us to make it to the church safely, I thanked him

for living in the United States of America, I thanked him for food

and shelter, I thanked him for a reasonable portion of health and

strength, I thanked him for life, liberty, and the pursuit of happiness,

I thanked him for family and friends, I thanked him for education,

experiences, and exposure, I thanked him for enemies and haters,

I thanked him for dying on the cross of Calvary and rising again

on the third day with all power in heaven and earth in his hands! I

thanked him for everything I could think of. Then I said I was sorry.

I was sorry for forgetting the purpose of gathering on Sundays. Sorry

for neglecting to worship Him in spirit and in truth. Sorry for acting

like it was all about me. In fact, when I got up from the floor, by the aid of very caring and concerned ushers, my husband was well into his sermon. I must have been down on that floor for all of thirty minutes, I'm sure!

They escorted me to the ladies room, still weak from prayer and praise. I raised my eyes to look sheepishly in the mirror so as to survey the damage. Well, for starters, my hair that had not long ago been neatly styled into place, was now, plastered to the side of my face, held there by a combination of tears, sweat, and other liquids from various orifices on my face. I managed to move it out of my eyes, unable to comb it as I did not have my purse with me. The hair I could handle, I just wanted to see my outfit.

Remember the Kelly green suit with the brown fur around the collar and the cuffs? Well, it now had dark brown streaks all down the front of it from my eyeliner and make-up. Remember those bad Kelly green pointed-toe sling backs with the brown wooden heel? Well, the pointed toes weren't so pointed anymore. You see, while face down on the floor, I had kicked and kicked until I had managed to re-configure the tips of the shoes into a weird accordion deal so that the Kelly green dye had been scuffed off and all that remained was off-white leather glaring out from the rest of the shoe! All I could say was "I look a mess." Just then as I was reaching for a Kleenex to begin the process of sprucing up, the Lord said to me, "You have never looked better. This is what I wanted all along. This is what I expect from you when you come into my house. I want a broken heart, a broken and a contrite spirit. I have never been interested in what you were wearing. This is my house. You are to enter into my gates with thanksgiving and into my courts with praise!" Again the flood gates opened. I began praising him all over again.

The ladies room became a sanctuary in and of itself. I got it. I would never again tell the Lord what I would and would not do in his house. I left that Sunday saying like the Psalmist, "Not unto us, not unto us, but to thy name be the glory!"

<u>Souvenir: I Samuel 16:7</u>

<u>"man looketh on the outward appearance,</u>

<u>but the Lord looketh on the heart."</u>

Life Lesson 17:

"The Wizard of Oz from God's Perspective" ("The Dorothy Complex")

℘

Some years ago, the Lord began speaking to me about the stories and fairy tales that are so engrained in our American culture. We learn them in school, we see them on television, and we even pay to see them acted out on stages and at movie theaters. While conducting some research about a particular fairy tale, I was surprised to learn that fairy tales are not unique to American society. They can be found in many different cultures around the world. One reason for this is because fairy tales contain what are often referred to as "universal themes" that are readily recognized and easily understood by peoples from all walks of life.

The Lord used something we are all familiar with to drive home deeper, spiritual truths concerning one story in particular: "The Wizard of Oz". We know the characters, we know the music, we know the story, yet the Lord gave fresh insight regarding them:

I. The Storm is Coming. When we first encounter Dorothy, she is busy working on the farm with her Auntie Em and Uncle Henry. While they are all busy carrying out their duties, we are introduced to farm hands and neighbors. Distracted, or perhaps bored, Dorothy stops performing her duties and begins to daydream and talk to her dog. She begins singing the song, "Somewhere over the Rainbow"; a testament to the fact that she longs to be anywhere but where she is currently. The lesson that the Lord drove home concerning this scene was: **"The importance of staying on task."** Dorothy lived in the part of the country that was known for tornadoes and dust storms. She should have been focused on the business at hand instead of longing to be elsewhere. She should have been preparing for the future. But while she is daydreaming, she doesn't notice the wind blowing; she doesn't see the leaves falling, the trees leaning, and the dust blowing. She fails to realize that a storm is coming. When we are distracted, it is easy to miss the obvious. While her family is hunkering down in the storm shelter, Dorothy is elsewhere, both mentally and physically. Worldly distractions often lead to spiritual subtractions.

II. **Coming out of the Storm.** When Dorothy's house touches down, she realizes that the storm has ceased and the wind has stopped blowing. Upon exiting her house, she notices the vibrant colors and beautiful surroundings. She remarks to To-To, "We're not in Kansas anymore." How right she is. The Lesson here is this: **"Your outlook is always different when you come through a storm."** You don't see things quite the same. Once you have survived what you thought you couldn't survive; once you live through it; once you make it, your perspective is forever changed. You quickly learn that some people are not at all what they appear to be. What she thought were flowers, were actually little people. Be careful. These little people begin celebrating her, because unknowingly, she has defeated their arch enemy, The Wicked

Witch. Another lesson is this: coming through the storm is hard. God knows we are vulnerable. We need to ask Him to surround us with real people who will love us and celebrate us; who will hold us while we heal, but will do so honestly and lovingly.

III. <u>Without Fail, She Meets a Man!</u> The first person Dorothy meets while out on the "road" is a man! It never fails. Men and boys are everywhere. Lesson: **"Don't fall for the first one who comes along!"** Look at him: He can't stand up straight, but Dorothy likes him anyway. Before long, they begin to converse. He begins scratching his head, she begins scratching hers. Something's not quite right. First of all, he can't stand up straight, and now she finds out he can't think straight, because he has no brain! He had **hang-ups** when she met him, but she **hooks up** with him anyway. Dorothy just makes one bad decision after another. Right here, we know that Dorothy has not been reading her bible, because if she had been, she would have remembered that we should "Let this mind be in you which was also in Christ Jesus." He can't keep his mind on anything if he doesn't have one!

IV. <u>All that Glitters is not Gold.</u> No, it might be tin. The Tin Man, that is. Dorothy and the Scarecrow now meet The Tin Man. Dorothy is altogether smitten with him. She is quite impressed. He's shiny. Dorothy begins to talk to him, too. Lesson: "**Don't judge a book by its cover.**" Before we fall head over heels for a man, do some investigating first. See what he is about. Through dialogue, Dorothy finds out that this man doesn't have a heart. Now, right there, Dorothy should have left him right where she found him. Everyone knows that if he has no heart, he has no love. Not only that, he cannot move! Stuck. Unable to move freely. He is lacking the oil of the Holy Spirit that will allow him to move. The Bible says, "Where the spirit of the Lord is, there is liberty!" He, clearly, is not the one, yet she hooks up with him, too.

V. <u>The Lyin'.</u> Who is the next person Dorothy meets out on the road? The Lion. He is the worst one of all. He *looks* ferocious! He *looks* scary! He's big! He's bad! He's a fake! He looks like he should be able to protect her. He looks like he should be able to provide for her. He looks like a lion, but in reality, he's doing nothing but lyin'! Lesson: **"Looks are often deceiving."** I am reminded of the fig tree that Jesus saw one day when he was hungry. It was during the time of year that figs **should have been** hanging from it. As Jesus approached it, he found no fruit on it, only leaves. For this reason, Jesus cursed it so that nothing grew on it ever again. There is a danger in merely *looking the part*. The Lord has great expectations for his people. If we only look the part, and are bearing no fruit, we are in danger of being cut off. Concluding lesson: Between the four of them, they were a sorry lot, indeed. We have Dorothy who was constantly searching for something; she was weak minded and unable to make good decisions. The Scarecrow: he had just too many hang-ups; he couldn't stand up for himself nor think for himself. The Tin man: All dressed- up and no place to go. Shiny, but no substance. Lastly, the Lion. Hypocritical. Scary. Weak. We have to stay in the Word of God to help us discern what company to keep, and which to dismiss. The answer to all of their problems could be found in one Scripture, found in the Word of God:

Souvenir: II Timothy 1:7

"For God has not given us the spirit of fear (Lion),

but of power (Dorothy), and of love (Tin Man),

and of a sound mind (Scarecrow)!

Life Lesson 18:

"The Trouble with Snow White" (A Biblical View of Snow White and the Seven Dwarfs)

I fondly recall speaking at a gathering of girls where I was able to share the profound spiritual truths found in the familiar fairy tale: Snow White and the Seven Dwarfs. Just as the Lord shared with me, I now share with you:

I. Her Situation. In an effort to get to know the character of Snow White, we need to check out her particular situation or life circumstances. We need to learn just what is really going on with her. When the story begins, if you recall, there is a woman talking to a mirror to whom she refers as "slave". So, we immediately get the sense that she is pretty important; maybe even powerful. But, we who are born-again know that "power belongs to God" (Psalm 62:11). Well, before long, she asks that very familiar question: "Mirror, mirror on the wall, who's the fairest of them all?" To her utter amazement, he answers back, and I paraphrase, "Well, it used to be you, but now there is one fairer than you." The queen is shocked. Lesson: As we get older, ladies, we need to ask the Lord to help us grow old gracefully. You had your turn. Get better, not bitter. Become a mentor and teach a younger woman the "ropes". Remember, every Mary needs an Elizabeth. Snow White is in a household with a woman who is jealous of her. She is also a part of a blended family. Sometimes fairytales depict blended families as dysfunctional and hateful. The truth is, all families are dysfunctional because all families are comprised of people! Fallen, depraved, sinful people. Whether one's family is the family of origin or the result of being blending together, every family needs Jesus!

II. Her Inclination. The word "inclination" means, "that which one is most likely to do in a given situation; our inward propensities; our knee-jerk responses; our initial reactions." Being this situation, what is it that Snow White is most inclined to do? The answer to this question can be discovered as we view her out on the veranda talking to the birds. She's cleaning up the patio with a ball gown on. We get a glimpse into the mind set of Snow White right here: She feels more comfortable talking to those outside her house than inside it. She begins singing the song, "someday my Prince will Come." Again, we encounter a young woman who is unhappy where she is and longs to be elsewhere. Lesson: When we feel unloved, unwanted, lonely, and misunderstood, we must run to the Word of God that ensures us "that *all* things work together for the good of them who love the Lord and are the called according to his purpose." She is inclined to daydream and sing about *some day* and *some man*. We need to deal with reality and trust God for the future.

III. Her Infatuation. An infatuation is defined as "something you like; that which you are impressed by; what stirs your emotions."

Lesson: We should always remember Colossians 3:12. It says, "If ye then, be risen with Christ, seek those things above…set your **affections** on things above, not on things on the earth." Through Snow White's sad situation, the Lord was showing me that infatuation grows out of one or two circumstances. It can either grow out of what one has ALWAYS seen or from what one has NEVER seen. For example, if a young girl's father has always been around, hard-working, paying bills, loving his wife, and taking care of his family, then a young woman will likely look for something similar in a mate, because this is what she has *always* seen. Likewise, if a girl's father has never been around; perhaps he was there, but was rather ambivalent toward her. Maybe he was apathetic and didn't seem to care one way or another. Or even worse, maybe displayed inappropriate affection toward her, then a young woman may likely look for something entirely different in a mate, because she has *never* seen it. In Snow White's case, we are never introduced to her father, only to her step-mother. Where was dad? What kind of father was he? There is a void in her life because of the absence of dad.

IV. <u>Her Desperation.</u> Later in the story, we find that things are going from bad to worse with Snow White. Now, her stepmother wants her dead. She has even commissioned a huntsman to kill her and as proof, she wants him to put her heart in a box and bring it to her. Ugh. As I looked at her gruesome request, I grew more and more perturbed with the stepmother. How presumptuous of her to assume that a woman's heart could fit in a box! I am reminded of the movie Titanic. As Rose recalls her experiences on the doomed ship, she says something most profound. She says, "A woman's heart is a deep ocean." I concur. Her children's cherished moments lie there, love, life and losses lie there. A woman's heart could never fit in a box! Physically, the heart is that organ that pumps blood throughout the body to ensure optimal function. While this is true, it is much more than that. According to Scripture, God says, "Guard the heart, for out of it flows the issues of life." All of the issues, all of the love, all of the promises kept and broken, all of the things that the heart has seen, how dare she think it could fit in a box! Desperation is defined as "a state of hopelessness; utter dependence on the kindness of others." It means to be at a loss; completely messed up; traumatized. Now, Snow White has no place to go. She has been chased into the woods...

V. Her Habitation. Habitation means "dwelling place." While in the woods, she comes to a cottage. She peeks through the window, knocks on the door, and lets herself in. In the real world, that is called Breaking and Entering and it could get you 3-5! Well, based on what she **sees**, she **assumes** all is well. She sees little chairs and a little table. She assumes that orphans live there because the house is in disarray. Lesson: Assumptions are dangerous. If you have not been invited in, don't assume you are welcome. My grandmother used to tell me, "Believe none of what you hear and only half of what you see." Better than that, there is the Word of God. Remember: "We walk by faith and not by sight." So, she says to herself, "If I clean up their house, they may let me stay." She was rendering her services for their good favor. This is dangerous because this would, essentially, make her beholden and indebted to them. She was, in essence, prostituting herself in hopes of compensating herself. You don't believe me,

I can tell. Well, what's that song they were singing when they came home from work...? And what would you say if you met a woman living with seven men—little or otherwise?! Joking aside, the beauty of her situation is that Jesus met a woman one day in a similar situation. She needed something, too. She needed some water. You remember, the woman at the well. Jesus said, "Where's your husband?" She replied, "I don't have one." He said, and I paraphrase, "You got that right, you have had many men, and the man you are with now, is not your husband, either." He did not despise her, he did not refuse her. He welcomed her. In her desperation, in her loneliness, Jesus welcomed her.

VI. Her Starvation. Well, in an effort to finally get rid of Ol' Snow, the queen figured she would just have to do it herself. It turned out that the huntsman had too much of a heart to kill her. So, the queen disguised herself as an old woman and convinced Snow White to let her in the cottage. As soon as she was inside, she showed Snow White an apple. A piece of fruit. Who does this sound like? Eve. Failed by the fruit! Lesson: The Lord showed me that we will eat anything when we're hungry enough. When there is a hunger that wants to be fed; a desire that refuses to be satiated, we will indulge. The flesh is a powerful thing and it takes a power greater than our own to overcome it's gravitational pull. As was the case with our foremother, Eve, so it is with Ol' Snow White: she ate and she died. Snow White ate because she was starved; starved for attention, starved for affection, starved for companionship, starved for relationship—she was just plain starved. She lacked the nourishment of a loving family, and as a result, she ate of the wrong fruit and she died. Lesson: There is a void in all of our lives that only the Lord Jesus Christ can fill. He is waiting with open arms to heal our diseases, fill our hunger, and redeem us back to the Lord God Almighty. We have examined a young woman's life. We have seen her sad **situation**; we have analyzed her **inclination,** and seen her unrealistic **infatuation**. We have gotten a glimpse of her sense of **desperation**; we have viewed her **habitation**, and we have focused on the result of spiritual **starvation.** When we find ourselves in any of these predicaments, we have only to remember that Jesus Christ is our only source of **salvation!**

Life Lesson 19:

"They, too, Believe"

Race relations being what they are in the United States of America, one would be hard pressed to find someone whose life has not been affected by racism, in some form or another. My life, unfortunately, has not been spared. I, too, have been negatively affected by the ubiquitous and insidious presence of racism in our country. One example in particular stands out.

I was six years old and in the first grade. Our class was making preparations for Christmas. The class smelled of gingerbread and candy canes. Garland made of popcorn and cranberries draped the beautiful Douglas Fir Tree that stood grand and tall in the center of our classroom. Boxes covered with shiny wrapping paper and big bows sat under our tree. Tiny lights hung from the windows and holiday cheer hung in the air like pleasant potpourri. It was beginning to look a lot like Christmas and we couldn't have been more excited!

On a certain day, we were coloring large pictures of Santa Claus. One little girl sitting next to me reached for the brown crayon to color Santa's face. I was intrigued! I had never seen a brown Santa before. "Why not?" I thought happily, my feet dangling happily beneath my seat. I reached for my brown crayon, too. Proud of our Black Santa Clauses, we smiled at each other. Coloring his hat and suit with equal amounts of zeal and vigor, we sung along with the Christmas carols playing softly in the background. As was her custom, our teacher walked around the room surveying the progress of our work. When she came to our table, she stopped and picked up my paper. The look on her face was serious and her icy stare seemed to cut right through me. Had I colored outside the lines? Did I forget to write my name on the paper? Was everyone else finished? Was I taking too long on this assignment? Suddenly panic replaced pride and I was petrified. The words she spoke dripped like venom from her lips. She opened her mouth and said, in a matter-of-fact- monotone, "Santa Claus is not Black. Everyone knows he is White. Please re-do it." I was deflated and humiliated. My ears were hot and my tears were, too. I just wanted to go home.

I am sad to say that this incident and several more besides, are as much a part of me as "steel-wheel" skates, Vacation Bible School, and pink bicycles with baskets on the handle bars. They are my life experiences and therefore, serve to form my psychological make-up; my schema, if you will.

So, while I was saved at an early age and learned to love God and the things of God in a loving home, the poison of racism had left powerful residue. Imagine my surprise when I won a four-year scholarship to a small Christian Liberal Arts College and was only one of a small percentage of Black students enrolled there. Mostly everyone was White. The people who worked in the offices were White. The majority of the students were White and most of the professors were White. A flood of emotions swept over me as my first day approached. I knew God had ordered my steps and miraculously opened doors for me to be there. I was most grateful for this opportunity to complete my four-year degree and begin my teaching career. I knew God had ordained this to be. But what would happen if the professors somehow misunderstood me? What if I misunderstood them? Were these people *really* Christians?

This was all new to me. My first college experiences had been on the campuses of Historically Black Colleges and Universities and I had been surrounded by people who looked like me. I had been instructed by professors who looked like me and I was *used* to people who looked like me. God was expanding my horizons, and I was not altogether sure how I felt about that.

I was enrolled in an Old Testament class. I was eager to learn; I've always been a good student. This particular day, the professor was teaching on Joseph. She asked the question, "Was there anything wrong with Joseph sharing his dream with his brothers?" Well, after an uncomfortable and absolutely unbearable period of silence, I just spoke right up and said, "No. Joseph's brothers were just jealous and they would have hated him no matter what." Pleased with my answer and fully expecting her to say something along the lines of,

"Flesh and blood has not revealed that unto you", I waited for her reply. She said, "Some things that the Lord speaks to you are just for you. They are not to be shared. They are for your ears and your spirit only. Joseph should not have shared information that only he and God were to be privy to." I lifted my hands in praise to God right there in that classroom. The tears filled my eyes and flowed like a river as I repeated, "Thank you, Jesus" over and over again. She had answered, in an instant, a question that had been on my mind for weeks. Instead of feeling like that frightened six year-old, I felt like I was in Bible Study at my home church! I felt the Spirit of the Lord there. I learned a very valuable lesson that day. Yes, I learned that Joseph should have kept his mouth shut concerning his future state. But it was more than that. That day, in a classroom located on a small Christian Liberal Arts College Campus, I learned that White people love Jesus, too! I learned that they, too, are my brothers and sisters. I learned that a petite Caucasian woman can rightfully divide the word of truth in such a way that chains are broken, questions are answered, the wounded are made whole, and God, himself is pleased! I learned that day that yes, White people believe in my

Life Lesson 20:

"How to Pull Down Strongholds"

℘

Strongholds are areas in our lives that are hard to conquer; hard to get over. They can be those sore spots that we don't want to talk about; those grudges we can't seem to get over or those dark places that haunt us when we are alone. Perhaps they are failures that sadden us or particular personality traits that seem to ruin opportunities for us. We all have them, we all know exactly what they are in our own lives. Having to come to this realization was a rude awakening for me.

I was sitting around the kitchen with my sisters-in-law and we began talking about some memories we all shared. We talked about church services, anniversaries, and the fact that children grow up all too quickly. Suddenly, someone said, "Yeah, remember that time when..." Before she started the story, I knew exactly where she was going. In an instant, I was quickly transported back to the day in question. Now, don't get me wrong, her story was not intended to single me out, and neither was she trying to openly embarrass me in front of the family. Nevertheless, I responded in a quasi-humorous tone, "I do *not* want to talk about that." I left the room.

I thought about it all the way home. I didn't say anything to anyone, but I was silently speaking to my Lord. It had been years since that particular incident and I thought I had "gotten alright" with it. Yes, it had been years, but no, I had not "gotten alright" with it. It still hurt. It still bothered me. I had merely placed a sterile psychological band-aid over it. A band-aid that, with the slightest tugging, would come right off and expose the wound, still bleeding, still ugly.

"Lord, help me." I cried in the silent hours when everyone in my house was asleep. "I thought I had given this to you, and I thought you had taken it. What is happening now? Why do I feel like this is happening all over again?" My Lord answered me; just like He always does. He spoke softly to my spirit and said, "Your inability to forgive is a stronghold. It is an area in your life that Satan has found to be of particular difficulty for you. He is using this vulnerable place to set up walls and to gain a foothold so that he will always be able to manipulate and maneuver your emotions. You cannot ignore it. You cannot simply try to forget it. No, my dear one, you have to pull it down!"

I held on to the Lord all night long. I wept and struggled. I cried and wrestled. By the morning, my eyes were puffy and I had a headache that wouldn't quit. Tired yet strangely energized, I knew what I had to do. I had to pull down those areas of unforgiveness that plagued my life. I had to somehow gain the victory over them so that I could go on unhindered and unrestrained. I had to… my spiritual life was in jeopardy. I had to pull down that stronghold. But how? The Lord led me to Scripture. Here, I found someone else who needed to pull down a stronghold. In the book of II Samuel 5: 1-10, there is the story of David and his army. It details what David had to do in order to win over his stronghold. This lesson blessed me so that I was able to use it, not only in my own life, but I was also able to bless a group of women over the course of a retreat weekend. The Lord showed me that there are four things we need to do in order to pull down strongholds in our lives:

I. **Identify the Enemy**. The Bible says in verse 6a that "David now led his troops to Jerusalem, to fight against the Jebusites." In this case, the enemy is clearly stated: It is the Jebusites. They are an enemy of God. (See Numbers 13:29 and Joshua 11:3). I am reminded of the fact that when you fight against a child of God, you are waging war against God, himself! God is Jehovah Nissi-the God who raises his banner in victory! He is a mighty battle ax; He is mighty in battle. He is Jehovah Sabaoth—He commands the hosts of angels and he does it on our behalf. The Jebusites were standing in David's way. We, as Christian women of today know, that "we wrestle not against flesh and blood but against principalities and powers, against spiritual wickedness in high places." Our enemy is Satan and we can defeat him the same way! Step #1 in pulling down the strongholds in our lives, is to identify the enemy.

II. Ignore their Expressions. Verse 6b illustrates this principle clearly. The Jebusites knew that David was on his way to attack them and they tried to insult him. Reading from the Good News Translation, it says, "You will never come in here, they told him, even the blind and lame could keep you out!" The Lord showed me that one of the most effective tools in the enemy's arsenal is to strike fear into the heart of the opponent. One of the best ways to do this is by using intimidation. Carefully chosen words that can cut with the precision of a surgeon's scalpel, can inflict much damage even before the first blow is thrown. So, it is here, with the Jebusites, they thought they were safe and secure, after all, they had been around in Moses' time. They had been around in Joshua's time and now here they are again, a seemingly invincible enemy, around in David's time. David wasn't the least bit deterred, he knew that the same God who delivered him out of the hand of the bear, the lion, and the giant, would deliver him out of the hand of the Jebusites. While the enemy was talking, David kept walking! No matter what the enemy says, we have to believe what God says! After all, whose report up to the gutter, and smiteth the Jebusites, and the lame and the blind, that are hated of David's soul, he shall be chief and captain." In essence, David was saying, "I have come to win. I will do whatever it takes to get the victory; even climb through the gutter." The *gutter*. This both blessed and broke me. God was saying to me that in order to get the victory, you will have to do the unthinkable. You will have to undertake an endeavor from which your heart shrinks back. You will have to go on a journey that both repels and scares you. You will have to do like Andy Dufresne, that battle weary character from the movie The Shawshank Redemption, and climb through the gutter. Although his was a physical gutter with years of human waste and refuse surging through underground pipes, the Lord said, "Your gutter will be no less repulsive. You will have to go back through the gutter of grudges, held much too long and much too closely." I cried. "You will have to dig through the filth of fake and phony forgiveness, and the pain of petty pretenses and immature ignorance." I cried harder. "You will have to trudge through the sewage of silent animosity; you must muddle through the muddy places of mediocrity and the piles of pride that have set up and hardened your heart." I pleaded with the Lord. He said I would have to go back through the dirt of denial and through the muck and the mire of too many years gone by. He said I would have to suffer through the stench of hard-heartedness and break through the bitterness that has held me back. Re-visit the places that I don't talk about in polite conversation. Surrender the things that others don't know about and would be shocked to find out about. Go back *to* the gutter. Go back ***through*** the gutter. The sewer. The underground places where you have allowed the enemy to take root. The only way you are to get the victory is to go there. You, Genea, will have to confront the stronghold and it is in the gutter! I was humiliated. I was hurt. I was challenged. I wanted to be changed. God assured me that when I did that; when I went back through the gutter, I would impact the environment. I would then be able to make a difference in this life for Him. I, like David, would be used mightily in his Kingdom. He assured me that when I finally gave it to Him, He would use my story for His glory! Step #3 is to impact the environment.

IV. Increase in the End. Verse 7b states, "…and he captured the stronghold of Zion, now called the city of David." Look what happened in the end: At the end of the day, when it was all said and done, what once had been called "The Stronghold of Zion" was now called "The City of David!" Because David was able to take control of what had been controlling them, he succeeded in the end. David was able to seize the strong hold, the secure place, the place that the enemy had been occupying for so many years. If you can take a good look at yourself and determine that you have to get the victory, you will! If you can get a hold of what has a hold on you, you will increase in the end. If you see that thing as destructive and deadly to your spiritual life, you will gain the victory! A stronghold is a strategic place in your life that the enemy has gotten himself into and he refuses to come down voluntarily. That's why you can't talk down a stronghold, you can't just wish it down, you can't just hope it down; you have to *pull* it down in the name of the Lord! It comes down through prayer, fasting, and meditating on the word of the Lord concerning that thing! This blessed me even more: The Lord shared with me that once you conquer that thing, whatever it is, you then, have the spiritual right to re-name that thing! It is not too late. The Lord says that He is able to restore unto us the years that the locust, the caterpillar, and the cankerworm have taken. **Once you re-claim it, re-name it!!!** For me, what was once called unforgiveness is now forgiveness. What was once a grudge is now compassion. What was once anger is now temperance. When we do it God's way, we can take back what the devil stole from us! When we do it God's way, we can't help but to increase in the end! The Bible says, "When a man's ways please God, he will make even his enemies to be at peace with him!" Through this very painful process, I have learned that greatness awaits those who are willing to go through the gutter to get it.

Souvenir: II Samuel 5:10

"And David went on and grew great

and the Lord God of hosts was with him."

Life Lesson 21:

"What To Do When They Don't Want You"

⚘

One of the most devastating blows of my Christian walk came several years ago, disguised as a most wonderful opportunity. I was asked to teach a class for a Bible College. Me. It was totally unexpected and I was thrilled! I felt woefully inadequate, though. You see, several years before, I *had* graduated from Bible College, but I had not earned a Bible Degree. I earned my degree in Liberal Studies, with a concentration in English Literature. I had also completed the Teaching Credential Program, in preparation to teach elementary school, not Bible College. In fact, I had taught Kindergarten and

First Grade for four years prior. So, my professional training, as you can see, prepared me to teach children. Could they really want me to teach adults? And teach them the *Bible*? Yes, I had been teaching the Women's Bible Study group at my church, and yes, I had been blessed to teach throughout the Bay Area and abroad, but a Bible College… really? This was waaaay outside my area of expertise.

As part of the interview process, I was contacted by phone and asked to dine with faculty members. It was at this time that particulars of the assignment would be given and where I would also have the opportunity to ask any and all questions concerning this new assignment. Though I ordered something, I could not eat a bite. I was so elated, that I simply soaked up all of the information given to me. They stated that my reputation as a sound Bible teacher preceded me. I was given a roll/record book along with the required text for the class. They told me they looked forward to working with me. That was it. With those words, I was off to make final preparations. I shouted all the way back home. "Thank you, Jesuses" were intermingled with the mandatory "Halelujah!" I had to be careful to keep my hands on the steering wheel and my eyes focused on the road, though they were constantly filling up with tears of joy.

The first evening of classes came. I was both excited and prepared. Though I had the roll book containing the names of my students, I looked forward to meeting them all face-to-face. They all filed in and I began my session. It was exhilarating! We talked! We shared! I gave out homework! It was great!

The second week came. I collected homework and began my session. Again, marvelous! One of the faculty members sat in the back of the class. Upon acknowledging his presence, he waved politely and left.

The third week came. We were really into the lesson and I could tell that they were "getting it". At the conclusion of the session, we had prayer, as was our custom. The Spirit of the Lord filled the room. We shouted and praised God like never before. It was awesome!

The following evening, I rushed inside my house to answer the phone. I could hear it ringing from the garage. We were just coming in from our weekly Bible Study classes at our church. I picked up the phone with a breathless "Hello?" I recognized the voice on the other end to be that of one of the faculty members from the college. After a bit of small talk, I received news that stung like an adder's bite. Apparently it had come to his attention and to the attention of others on the staff, that instead of "teaching", what I was actually doing was more along the lines of "preaching" and they would appreciate it if I would "stay in the pocket". Dumbfounded, I asked, "Is the information I am teaching doctrinally sound?" To which he responded, "Yes." Still confused, I asked, "Was there anything in particular that you observed the evening you sat in on my class?" He said, "No, but we would just prefer you "stay in the pocket." Vexed, I responded, "Stay in *whose* pocket? Since there seems to be nothing wrong with my ***information***, then you seem to have a problem only with my ***presentation***. Perhaps if you had actually observed my teaching presentation prior to hiring me, this conversation would scarcely be necessary." He went on to say that he was not "asking me to leave", but he was asking me "to change". Stunned, I simply stated that I would be returning the supplies to him the next day and thanked him for the opportunity. I further informed him that I was not interested in staying in "anyone's pocket."

I hung up the phone. Wounded, I wept. Wounded, I wondered. There was nothing wrong with my doctrine. I was teaching directly from the Word of God. There was nothing wrong with my ability to clearly communicate to my students. It was simply my personal teaching style. It wasn't *what* I was teaching, it was *how* I was teaching it! It was about my style. It was personal. They simply didn't want *me*.

In the weeks that followed, I received many wonderful phone calls from my students. Some were heart-felt inquiries as they wondered where I was. They expressed their confusion and displeasure. All gave words of encouragement, letting me know that my labor was not in vain. I was grateful for such words, they strengthened me.

It was awkward for a while. I love teaching and was really enjoying teaching *that* class. It was not easy, but I have since put it behind me, but not before gleaning in the Lord's field and gathering handfuls on purpose:

I. **"Favor" does not mean "Flavor".** Just because you are favored by God, it doesn't mean that you will be favored by people. It doesn't mean that you will be well received in every situation. You will not be everyone's "cup of tea". The Lord showed me that the reason Baskin-Robbins has been such a successful ice cream franchise is because there are 31 different flavors from which to choose. Not everyone will choose the same flavor! In other words, not everyone will like you and your particular brand or style. Not everyone will be impressed with you and not everyone will "get" you, so "get over it"! Ouch.

The Lord was teaching me through this very hard lesson that He is a God of variety. He let me know that the reason the oceans are so large is so that they can accommodate all sorts of creatures; the halibut and the hammerhead; the salmon and the sea urchin; the oyster and the octopus. They all fit; they are not the same, but there is room for them all! He also showed me that the reason gardens are so beautiful is because both the lily and the lavender can grow there; the rose and the rhododendron; the daisy and the dandelion. There is room for them all! Finally, he drove the point home when he showed me something in the way he chose his disciples. He chose 12 men;

men with different personalities, different temperaments, and different vocations. They were different, but he chose them none the less. They did not do things the same way, but he still chose them. So, it is with us, the people of God, we are not all the same. The Lord was saying, "Just do what *you* do, your gift will make room for *you!*"

I am reminded of a young King David. Though he had been anointed king of Israel, he was, at this time, serving King Saul. The taunts and intimidations of Goliath of Gath had come to David's attention and he asked of Saul permission to go and fight him. Saul tried his best to convince David that he should not do this because he was *just* a lad and that Goliath had been training for battle *since* he was a lad. Seeing that David was undeterred, Saul offered him his very own armor with which to fight Goliath. Perhaps not wanting to seem ungrateful, David tried on the armor. It did not fit; it was obviously too large and cumbersome and simply would not do. David, as respectfully as he could, said, and I paraphrase, "Thank you very much, O King, but I can't use your armor. I may not do it like you do it, but just give me a chance." We don't all accomplish the same goal in the same way, but by the grace of God, we can complete that which is assigned to our hands.

II. <u>When a Good Door Closes, a Better Door Opens.</u> Since that experience, God has done exceedingly, abundantly above all that I could ever ask or think! He has allowed me to speak in places I never would have imagined. He has allowed me to be in the company of great men and women. Over and over again, he proves the Scripture to be true: "Power belongs to God!" I will not pretend to have come through that experience unscathed, but I have come through it unashamed. I can resolutely say in the words of the Great Apostle Paul, "I am not ashamed of the gospel of Jesus Christ, for it is the power of God unto salvation." God has done great things for me and I am determined to tell it wherever I have opportunity. One other lesson I have learned through that experience was that yes, your *gift* will *make* room for you, but it is your *lift* that will *keep* room for you! Let me explain: The Lord was showing me that your gift will get you in the door, but it will be your lift; the constant lifting of your hands in praise; the constant lifting of your voice in thanksgiving, and the constant lifting of your eyes unto the hills, that will *keep* doors opening for you!

Having come through this painful period, there is one more lesson that stands out above all the rest. This lesson has become a hallmark of my life. I no longer question where the Lord leads me, nor why he leads me there. I no longer shrink back from opportunities or assignments. I am no longer disappointed when things don't seem to "work out". I am learning to walk by faith and leave the details to my omniscient, omnipresent, omnipotent, and omni-competent Father who has my best interest at heart!

III. Ask the Lord for a "Spider's Spirit". In the book of Proverbs 30:24-28, the writer shares some fascinating information with us. He explains that there are four animals in the world that are small, but they are very, very wise. He lists the ant, the conie, and the locust, in verses 25-27. But the one that the Lord used to speak directly to my storm-tossed soul during this time, is found in verse 28: the spider. Of the spider, the writer says this:

"The spider taketh hold with her hands, and is in kings' palaces." The Lord used this illustration to speak peace to me. He says the spider moves purposefully and deliberately. She is elusive and quiet. No one knows just how and when she makes her entrance, but there she is, nevertheless! She makes no noise; no announcement; yet her presence is unmistakable. She is equally at home in the shack of the pauper as well as in the palaces of kings.

God was saying that just like the spider, you must be absolutely focused on what it is you are supposed to be doing, regardless of the setting. He went on to say, you will be able to address a Sunday School class with the same preparation and power as you would the great crowds in a convention hall; and do so with equal parts humility and grace. You will take every assignment seriously and take hold of it with fierce intensity. He was saying, "Don't be surprised, Genea, when you, like the spider, look up and find yourself in king's palaces!" Stay focused. Be deliberate. Remain a woman of purpose. It has come at a great price, but I thank the Lord for my "Spider Spirit!"

<u>*Souvenir: Romans 8:28*</u>

<u>*"And we know that all things work together for good to them that*</u>

<u>*love God, to them who are the called according to his purpose."*</u>

Breinigsville, PA USA
02 March 2010
233424BV00001B/43/P